Captivated

· · · · · · · · · · · · · · · · · ·

Lyrics of an Overflowing Heart

~ Thomas E. Brock ~

ISBN: 978-0-6151-3513-7

Dedicated to she who gave me no choice but to love her. May her life be as blessed as mine has been for having had her in it.

Table of Contents

Dedicated to she who gave me no choice but to love her. May her life be as blessed as mine has been for having had her in it.

Table of Contents

If My Kisses

If my kisses win not thy heart
And their hunger whet not thine own
If their fire inflame thee not
And their passion arouse not thy soul

Then there beats not
Within thy breast
A human heart

For I would woo thee my maiden
With sweetest honeyed kisses
Alive with love so impassioned
With tenderness so exquisite

That no mortal could endure
The fervor of my touch
And fail to succumb
To the wooing
Within my kiss

Time and Eternity

In that quiet space
Between the folds of time and eternity
Where mere words no longer suffice
We shall gaze upon each other rapt

In that pristine place
Amidst the crystal light of eternal morn
Where any spoken word must fail
All fades to black save you and me

And there where immortality gently rests
Secure within galvanized glance
We shall speak a language all our own
That silently transcends mere words
And language spoken that no longer can suffice

In that quiet space
Between the folds of time and eternity

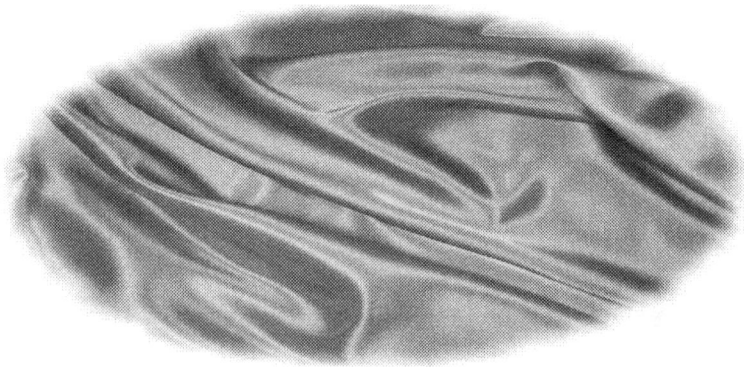

Heart At Peace

How do I begin to tell the tale
When the words that would elucidate
How this raging torrent leaves my heart
A cataract franticly, madly cascading
Do not exist in mortal tongue?

How can a single, silent glance
Speak the story of a lifetime
And unleash thoughts voluminous
And desires . . . and needs
That no earthly substance can sate?

How can an innocent, bashful smile
Etch eternal writ of ownership
With blood's insoluble bonds
And imprison securely a heart
That has never before been chained?

How can a dainty, lithesome maiden
Surround the impregnable fortress
And devastate the armies defending
My well-guarded heart without so much
As a word or arm lifted in battle?

How can this timid, fragile lass
So effortlessly leave naked
And dangling in the breeze
My heart which no other could touch
As if it were hers to bare?

I have not answers any more
Save to whisper her name
For merely having that sweet name
Skip and laugh thru the playground of my mind
Brings balance to my reeling world

I have not desires any more
Save to be captive in her gaze
For I know that only then
When I am reflected in her eyes . . .
Only then is my heart at peace

Full Tender

Across the room her eyes find mine
By accident or by design?
It matters not for she seems to know
That she has dealt a fatal blow
That she has complete control
Over my now enchanted soul

Indeed she revels in her mastery
Without a word . . . taunting me
With unspoken promises teasing me
O silent exquisite agony!

In awestruck wonder gratified
Every desire sated, satisfied
My heart's protective cover blown
Will absconded - no longer my own
Your price, my love, I surrender
My captive heart as full tender

Speak Softly Love

Speak softly, love
For the ears of my heart
Are finely tuned to thee

Every whisper, every sigh
That from thy lips escapes
Loudly peels within
Its inner chamber walls

Every subtle gesture
That plays upon thy face
Speaks volumes within my soul
Strongly sewn to you

Yes, your softest sound
Or slightest signal
Rules me heart and soul

Speak softly, love

Silent Caresses

(Shakespearean Sonnet)

My eyes alit upon the maiden fair
Celestial angel hid in human guise
She meets my gaze upon the dreamy air
Impassioned kisses mix with breathless sighs

Across the room's tumult of crowded noise
Amidst the maze of twisted legs and arms
Exquisite agonies; enraptured joys
Both wend their way - unspoken fatal charms

Caresses silent calm my secret fears
As gently lifting opaque outer veil
Who, what, where - nonessential – disappears
Our very essence shared in full detail

Two souls unite that instant 'neath the sun
Forevermore, two hearts shall beat as one

Captivated Maiden

(Acrostic)

Call to me fair maiden
Awaken this sleeping prince
Plant a stirring in my heart
Trace your name within –
It awaits your loving scribe
Veneer your claim in gold
Adorn it with diamond sparkles
This treasury of love
Everlasting happiness
Doth await thee maiden fair

Meet me in eternity
Assuage my deepest fears
Ingrain your heart in mine
Dance with me upon the stars
Eternity captivated
Now within our grasp

Blushing Moon

Blushing Moon
Embarrassed
Blows blanched rays
Downward
Illuminating
The darkest recesses
Of my heart
Now rekindled
Burning brightly
Radiant

Empress of the midnight skies
She rules my imprisoned heart -
The treasure she keeps
Hidden there
Locked
Within the dungeon
Of her nocturnal realm

She holds sway
Over the tides of my heart
Ebb - by this queen - vanquished
By her order, all is flow

She soars
Across the starlit sky
My soul captive with her sails . . .
Whispering
Sweet surrender in her ears -
Blushes
The princess primeval
At my incessant doting

Moon is full tonight
Wandering creature of light
Fill my soul with luminous delight

I shall mourn the light of day
As it takes my love from me
Until the sun shall set
And I with blushing moon
Shall rise again

Dancing Upon A Moonbeam

We danced upon a moonbeam
Ecstasy upon a darkened stage
Sailed upon a surging sea
Transcending temporal realms
Philosophy of affectation
Hanging by a tortured thread
Advent of adulation
Love at last arrived

Ebony Veil

In the dreamy side of sunset
As moon climbs silvery steps
Adoring star after adoring star

Until at last she rests
On her advantageous perch
The window sill from which
She peeks into the other side of night

Gathering leftovers of the day
That she may filter the ebony veil
With gentle caresses
To light her shadowed realm

In that dreamy side of sunset
You will find my heart
Wrapped within the lace of love
Offered upon satin sighs
Upon the illumined vessels
Of Nox's eternal lamp

For somewhere under this ebony veil
This primordial orb of night
Traces gentle outlines
Upon the lovely curves
Of my true love's fairest face

And though distance does its damage
Hiding her from my straining eyes
I imagine my captive heart
Traversing these golden threads
Until it finds its way home
And rests upon the bosom
That has stolen it from me

For as surely as moon rules the night
So she rules the darkest regions of my heart
Bringing to light colored sensations
With the warmth of true love's glow

And in this dance called life
Each moonbeam is but my heart
Dropping feathery forget-me-nots
To adorn the one who owns the heart and soul
Of this captivated, enchanted knight

I cried today

She sat there
Calmly speaking
Words that squeezed
Heart sprung flow
Thru these salty sieves
I call eyes

Though I tried
I could not
Keep the fruit
Of her words
From dampening
Harvest

When she said
She'd give up
Her beloved Fender . . .
To be with me!

I cried

* A Fender is an electric guitar

Enchantress
(Double Acrostic)

Elixir of lov**e**
Nectar of heave**n**
Chocolate aphrodisia**c**
Heavenly flouris**h**
Azure eyes of nirvan**a**
Nymph from Ede**n**
Trellis of my hear**t**
Rose of splendo**r**
Essence of paradis**e**
Symphony of happines**s**
Salvific goddes**s**

Lines On Your Face

Lines on your face don't bother me
They are but the keeper of time
And each line gained in my company
Is but a reminder of how blessed I have been
To have lived that line with you

Lines on your face don't bother me
Though they seem to win the game
Your heart beating so close to mine
Beats ever truer, stronger
As each line appears

Lines on your face don't bother me
For time will claim its victory
But never can it dim nor diminish
The ever blossoming fragrance
Of these two hearts so in love

Lines on your face don't bother me

Inspired by the opening line to Nora Jones' "I've Got To See You Again".

Late Have I Found Thee

Late have I found thee
Yearning of my life
Nectar of my soul
Narcotic of my heart
Essence of ecstasy
Tapestries of light
Terraces of joy
Emissary of enchantment

Matters Not

I cast a bucket of pearls into the sea
Watching as they frolicked in the frothy brine
Laughing and gurgling til one by one
They faded into the depth's murky blue

I threw a thousand whispers into the wind
And listened as they cavorted in the breeze
Caroming and echoing recklessly
Scattering wildly as they waned ethereal

I catapulted golden coins over the rainbow
Amused as they climbed clanking upon arched hues
Until sliding down shoots of green and red and blue
They filled leprechaun's proverbial pot

I launched a full quiver of sunbeams into midnight
Arrows of light dispersed into the pitch
Side by side kissing softly in flight
Until dimming slowly, they succumbed to night

And in the dulled darkness I sit
Penniless and plain in the silent void
For with you what need have I of more
Without you . . . all else matters not

Light of Life

The sun is nothing
When you radiate upon my life

The stars but fizzling fireflies
When your eyes dazzling spark

The new moon but a dulled shadow
When your smile bewitches the night

The sunset but a dampened match
When your lips ignite fireworks

Me and You

The world's greatest poets each made endeavor
To capture love and beauty forever
Homer to Virgil to Shakespeare . . . beyond
Each has employed his inked magic wand
To pen phrases of honeyed description
Upon the object of his happy affliction

Helen and Grace Kelly and Princess Di
A sunset painted on a summer sky
Diamonds and emeralds and rubies
Among earth's most beloved beauties
And each has had their place in verse
By poets whose path I unworthily traverse

Samson and Delilah, Romeo and Juliet
And other famous lovers we all have met
Even nature provided the life-mating dove
As manifestation of endless love
And these loves also are well recorded
With verse which poets renowned awarded

And while I am not so bold as to claim
Equal footing with these men of fame
For my verse to theirs is as burlap to linen
It covers warmly . . . but abrases the skin -
Coleridge and Tennyson and Keats had not
What I have been given but could never have bought

For they wrote of mere beauty my darling dear
While I . . . I write of you - beauty without peer
And though they spoke glowingly of lovers true
They spoke of **nothing** . . . *compared to me and you*

O Awaken

O rise and shine my darling!
O awaken my gentle queen!

Let me kiss the sleep from your dreamy eyes
Let me tease the moonbeams from your trellised hair
Let me trace the satin of your impassioned skin
Let me silhouette the valley of your hallowed neck
Let me lavish ruby upon your quivering lips

Nay! Let me linger awhile by my sleeping angel
Nay! Let me in wonder gaze upon my dreaming princess

O rise and shine my darling!
O awaken my gentle queen!

On Bended Knee

Far and wide my fame had spread
Mighty knight astride thoroughbred
Evil's minions blanched and fled
Before my sword of righteous dread

Everywhere that I spread redemption
Stomping evil and dissension -
Rich and poor made reverent mention
Of one whose beauty defied comprehension

Fairest of flowers and thrice as pure
Gracious queen gentle, demure
No longer can my heart endure
Surely it succumbs to her allure

In haste I ride to meet her
She of whom all folk concur
She who makes my soul to stir
She who my affections doth incur

At last! She comes into sight!
More radiant than pure light
Overpowering, sheerest delight
My senses desert in euphoric flight

In awe I sink to the floor
She measures not her fame - but more
I must! But dare I implore
To serve this angel I adore

Enthralled I approach my lady
Humbly, trembling on bended knee
Fearing this bedazzling beauty
Would judge me unworthy

Can she tell I cower at her feet?
This knight who has never tasted defeat
Cannot find the strength even to greet
She who makes his heart miss its beat

Without word she unsheathes my sword
Gladly I die than be ignored . . .
Why kneeleth thou, my noble lord?
Stand. Thou hast my heart - thy deserved reward

Solitary Kiss

Tis I, fairest maiden
Come to woo thee truly
Weary not thy feet
Nor sully thy garments
In these greening fields
Nay! Ride upon my steed awhile
As befits such a noble
Queen.

And I thy servant
Shall accompany thee on thy way
At thy precious feet where I belong
For I am truly thy servant
Eternally.

And if I please thee
When this day is o'er . . .
If I may be so bold . . .
Perhaps thou wouldst deign
To grant me eternal bliss
With the raptures embodied
In a single, solitary
Kiss . . .

Solitaire

Patiently waiting
In the ebony stillness
A bare dance floor

Silently
In the dark
His hand takes hers

One man
One woman
Move together

Soundless
Rapt radiance
Sparkling in the night

There could be no other
. . . man
. . . woman

For the slow, stately
Hushed setting
Of this solitaire

Wondrously

What a perfect dream you are . . .
With windblown tresses cascading
In quiet adoration
About blushing cheeks
And blooming lips

How deeply I dream of you
The sun about which
My night times revolve
Orbiting full circle
But ever facing you

How you blow thru the chasms
Of my craggy, windswept heart
Tickling every ridge and valley
Eliciting a full chorus
Of loving sighs

How you cascade
Thru the life-blood
My heart pumps
As it courses
Throughout the rivers
Of my continent
Feeding every tributary
Until every cell is steeped
In you

How every cell of my being
So thoroughly filled
Cannot help but adore you
Their sole remaining reason
For existence

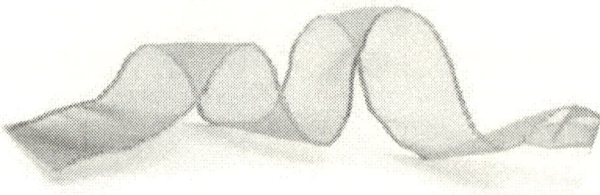

How they blush
At the thought
That for even
The slightest
Moment –
YOU
Would indulge them
With your presence

How wondrously
My whole being
Blooms
Every instant
You are
Near

Snowflake and Lava

Like a snowflake
On a summer day
I am without your love
Certain to melt away

Like molten lava
In a winter's gale
My life without your touch
Becomes brittle, frail

Like morning dew
Meets its fate
Without you life's joys
Soon evaporate

Like a butterfly
Caught in the wind
Without you my anchor
I meet an untimely end

Like a seashell
Swallowed by the sea
Without you to succor me
I succumb to obscurity

Like a tortoise
Crossing that fateful road
My heart without your kiss
Is flattened under heavy load

For what am I
Without your love
But the nothingness
You redeemed thereof

Tin Man

What have you done with my heart?
You mesmerized with your smile
Enchanted with your glowing soul

With my defenses safely disarmed
By your dazzling treachery
Brazenly you plucked my prized jewel

In its place you've left
This squeaky mess of pumping tin
To hide your lover's larceny

Now I walk among the living
Attempting to hide the masquerade
This drone as man enacts

I know my heart now stolen
Will never leave its captor thief
There is but one cure for this metal man

Surrender thine own heart
To fill this empty cavity of my chest
Else forever the tin man, I remain

Taken For Granted

Will you take me for granted
Will you always presume

Whatever you desire
Will you simply take
Without second thought
Without asking . . .
What *I* might like

Will you do these things . . .
For me . . .
Will you?
Please?

Just once . . .
I would discover love
So deeply woven
Into the very fiber
Of the canvas of my life

That though you *demand*
It is not disregard but surety -
Confidence so unshakeable
It manifests as command
To those who could not . . .
Understand

That though you take without asking
Whatever of me you desire
It is in the knowledge
Your happiness is the only thing
That brings joy to my heart

For never could I settle for love
That did not so permeate
The very blood coursing thru our veins
That you would take me for granted . . .

You Ask

You ask for my thoughts . . . Thoughts?
Between these ears there are no thoughts
Only spirals of loving glimpses
Only teasing tendrils of memories
Of you

You ask about my home . . . Home?
Ascend the stairway of my heart
You need no knock nor key
You should know it well
For my heart, my home abides
In you

You ask if you are beautiful . . . Beautiful?
All others are but fireflies flitting furiously about
As if by being frantic enough
They could compare to you
The midday sun

You ask how much I love you . . . Love?
Look into my eyes and tell me
If you see not a soul you have set free
No longer encumbered by the shackles of this world
Soaring high enough to touch divinity
For only there might it find rest
At your feet

There

There
Deep within -
Beyond
The boundaries
Of my very soul

There
In places
Within my being
Hidden from me -
Until now

There
Have you burrowed
Surely
Truly
Unerringly

There
Planted your flag
Of conquest
In my being's
Granite core

There
In virgin soil
Hitherto
Untrampled
Unplowed

There
Grown roots
Secured
The ethereal strands
Of eternity

There
Awakened need
Incessant
Hungering
Thirsting

There
Creatures of my soul
With gaping mouths
Upturned
Demand to be fed

There
Desperate
Dying
I wait -
For you

Serendipity

Cluttered clouds gently joust
Upon blueberry fields above
Choreographed calligraphy
Entertaining youthful hearts

Longed legged asters merrily
Do-sa-do with wide-eyed daises
White and purple poetry
In the lavender breeze

Setting sun's twilight twang
Of crickets' rosined bows
Evening time serenade
Welcomes the dreamy dusk

Somnolent sailor riding high
Smoky sun o'er ocean pitch
Shimmery snowflakes
Of sifted candle light

Two enchanted lovers loll
Cherry blossom captive hearts
Osculating orchids
Pristine petals of pleasure pure

Softly embracing a lazy day
Within a lilac frame
Discovered serendipity
Another Saturday memory

Save My Soul

Like a favorite memory from a forgotten dream
You made your entrance - a vision radiant
Newly reappeared to save from itself my soul
No one has ever drunk so deeply of this soul
Evicting fears long sewn into its very lining
Terrified you are but illusion of my hungering heart
Tantalizing torment in idyllic perfection
Even now, I gasp at your desire to make me your own

Slain

Mighty is the warrior
Facing me on the battlefield

Moments earlier
I strode into battle
Confident in my plated armor
So surely seated
Upon my sturdy frame
Proud in the strength
Of my granite-hewn arms
Wielding my fierce Olympian sword

Now - as my adversary approaches
A shadow of doubt tempts my resolve

Closer now! I can see the eyes!
Steeled with invincibility
Armed with arrogance and disdain
They penetrate my very being
With a terrible thrust
So sure, so devastating
It shudders me to my core

My defenses breached
So effortlessly
Sure sign of my pending fate
My armor now but weight
To hold me anchored here
Unable to escape my doom
At the sword of this
Titanic gladiator

Too late!
Have I realized
No match am I to this
Conquering champion
This is no battle
Tis but a hunt
And I the desired prey

With a fell swoop
Of a lethal lance
I am brought to my knees
My heart opened and exposed
Torn and gushing red
It pours out its life force
For all the world to see

Mortally wounded
The world dizzy and spinning
Stubbornly I open my eyes
For one last look at this world
Determined to meet death unyielding

No room for mercy
Upon the battlefield
The conqueror nonpareil
Closes for the final thrust

And so plants upon my trembling lips
Fairest maiden
Slaying
With her
Kiss

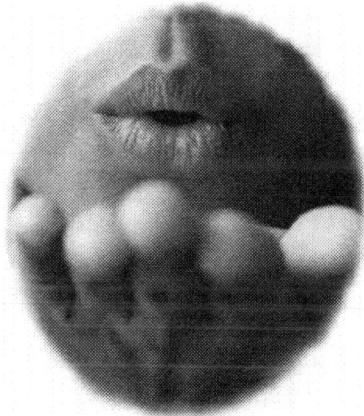

Sing To Me

Sing to me my muse
Dreamy honeyed notes
Caress inspired visions
Delight imaginings

Surround a lover's sortie
Besiege this fortressed heart
Claim my prized possession
Exact rapture's full ransom

Serenade my sapphire soul
Thrill with whispers dulcet
Elicit in the satin air
Silken reveries repose

Ravish amorous ears
Tempt with cherished tongue
Your silken sighs seduce
Longings of a captive heart

Sing, with lavish voice
Impassion sumptuous spark
O beloved six-stringed siren
Steal my wistful soul

With aphrodisiac of angels
Satisfy this thirsting spirit
Serenade with holy nectar
Sate this starving soul

I close my eyes but cannot hide
From the beauty of your song
Ecstatic faltering
Hopeless capitulation

You play upon velvet strings
Fixed within my heart
Fragrant symphony of passion
Resounding harmony

Lacy aria essence
Hymn of enamoring kiss
No longer able to refrain
Succumb to your enchantment

Yes! Sing with me my maiden
Intone dulcet melody
Sing duet enchanted
Sacred affectation of love

When I Awake
(Monchielle)

When I awake to you
Mid dewy mist of morn
Stars in your ebon eyes
Cascading - light the skies
Rival morning sunrise

When I awake to you
And feel the languid beat
Of your heart next to mine
As sun scales soft skyline
Time to timeless entwine

When I awake to you
Submerged within your smile
So serene, gentle, pure
Atop mountain grandeur
Eternities endure

When I awake to you
And you whisper my name
Upon silvered seashore
Waves of blessedness soar
Echo forevermore

Satin Beat

Join me in a love song
Lips in rhythm; hearts in perfect tune
Let's play a silky beat
Upon the instrument of life

May I have your hand
Upon the floor of destiny
We glide together slowly
In a dance for only two

Two lives waltz together
Two hearts beat a single note
One song sung sultry sweet
Forever together our satin beat

Thief Primordial

You have stormed the gates
Guarding my castle walls
Razing all that would resist
Laying waste with ease

You have defeated the sentry
Keeping watch upon my heart
Lifeless testament
To your victory complete

Inside where I cannot hide
You have found me
And claim my very soul
A trophy to grace your mantle

I am locked out; looking in
Wondering where and how I might again
Gain entry to the heart and soul
I once claimed as mine
Foolishly thinking there might yet be hope

I have no mind left at all
I am but an ocean of emotions
That swell and toss and cast themselves
Upon your shoreline

Hungrily calling your name
As they swash upon the sand
Seeking desperately
Some trace of your step -
Proof that you are near

Through and through
You own that I treasure most
Yet so strong your sway
You may keep my treasure

Whilst I spend eternity
Following in your shadow
For but a glimpse of you
My thief primordial

Embodiment of Love

Lodestar of the ages
Yield of the heavens
Necklace of sacred joys
Nascent of paradise
Earthen goddess of radiance
Temple for my affections
Tabernacle of divinity
Embodiment of love

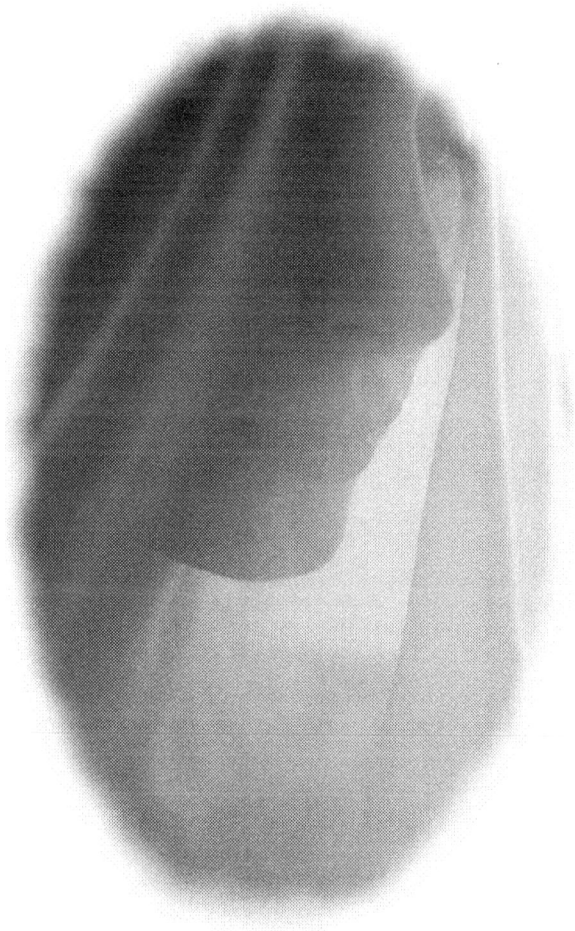

Distilled

Take the earnestness
Of my love for you
Stir in a heavy dose
Of the burden of loving
Someone so profoundly
As to be left trembling
In joy, in agony
Squeeze firmly until it bleeds
And you are left with
My tear

Take the fear of
Not being exactly
What you need
Everything you ever desired
Or dreamed
As you are to me
Feel it crush you
Under its weight
And you are left with
My sigh

Take all the bliss
In the world
Every happy, joyous moment
Every instance of ecstasy
Combine into a delicate flower
Place it to your lips
And you have my kiss

Take every touch
That ever spoke love
From one to another
Place it in a rainbow
Distill its purest essence
And you can at least imagine
My caress

Take every song of love
That ever stirred the air
Every heart that ever missed a beat
At a loved ones expense
Sprinkle a generous portion
Of angel dust
And simmer a hundred years
To approach my love

What Love Is This?
(Greensleeves melody)

What love is this which fills my heart
Which saves my soul from despair
What angel comes to my defense
An answer to my prayer
This! This! Is my true love
Who nestles close within my arms
Hush! Hush! My maiden sleeps
While I adore her fair charms

How came she in my darkest hour
How heard my silent pleading
When all was lost my seraph came
Stemmed my heart's grievous bleeding
Praise! Praise! Her healing touch
Restored my health with life anew
How! How! Can I thank her
Who all my hopes did renew

When my life on earth is over
I'll remember this blest day
And thank the Lord for this great gift
This maiden fair sent my way
Thanks! Thanks! For my darling
My loving queen I enthrone her
Joy! Joy! She joins her life
Our hands entwined forever

Tender Flame

Merrily the breeze skipped and danced
As it coursed thru flowered meadows
And we chased it and fell laughing
As I gave you a fresh-picked rose

We walked while water
Swashing gently wet the shore
Washing sand between our toes
Before retiring to sea once more

Thru straws we sipped soda
Topped with froth, sweet with wet
While waning with brilliant purple
And orange and red, the sun slowly set

Swaying slowly within the soft beat
We danced enthralled in the dark
The world fading to distant black
Victim of our igniting spark

We sat in silence hushed
Alone in the theatre of night
Sharing the serene celestial show
Under stars' silvered light

With surreal beams cascading
We kissed in the moonlight
Swooning, we dared to hope
The sun would never catch the night

And so closes a day with my love
A day I find myself unworthy of
Yet I hope my remaining days bring the same -
Me and my love sharing love's tender flame

Life Savings

Yesterday like the wind
Has rustled thru the leaves
Then softly withered away
As if it had never been

Tomorrow like a salesman
So full of promise
But without guarantee
It will ever come to be

Yesterdays perhaps
Were wonderful
Tomorrows may be
Unforgettable

But we cannot spend
What we do not have
What we have is now

I would spend
My life savings
With you

How Much

You ask how much I love you . . .

I come to you humbly
Unassuming, unembarrassed, unashamed
In the naked knowledge
That I would be yours and no others

No words can tell the story
Of the love I bear for you
But imagine if you can . . .
The love in every love poem
You've ever read
The pain of every heartbreak
Of which you've ever heard

Sum them all together -
A thousand times over
And you will have
The barest beginning of a glimpse
Of the passion spilling from my heart
For you

There is no yesterday
Worth remembering
Except those few pages
With your name inscribed
There is no tomorrow
Worth imagining
Unless penned
By my life's ink
Held within your hand

For now that I have drunk
Of the cup of your love
Nothing else can satisfy
Nothing else ever quench
The insatiable thirst
Awakened
In the depths of my soul
By you

Consumed

Consume
I must consume you
Every morsel
Be consumed by you
Every last iota I call myself

For if any part of me
Be not joined
Fused to you
Irrevocably
Then speak not to me
And expect answer
For already I am a dead man

There beats within this chest
A tender, sensitive heart
Its every beat passionate
Quick to feel and profoundly
Delicate and slow to heal
It is all I have
I have placed it gently
Into your hands
Keep it well

I have been to the fabled mountain
Gazed unabashedly
Upon the shores of heaven
I have been to the well of wishes
And drunk deeply of forever
I have been to the sea of evermore
And without blanching dove full in

You the lilting butterfly
And I thy rocky fortress
Secure within my chambers
Ascend with me into the heavens!

There undisturbed by the rest
Of a meaningless world
I might cherish your purity
Serve you ceaselessly
Worship you among the stars
As befits you my goddess

And though I be not worthy
There tenderly, exquisitely
In eternal embrace
As gently as a snowflake alighting
I would dare to kiss you
The angel I adore

So in the midnight sun
We would cast our shadow
Entwined as one
Until it blackened
All the heavens and echoed
Into the farthest reaches
Of eternity

This Moment

Who can claim to know . . .
When love will serenade with sweet song
Where two paths converge and travel on as one
Which two will meld into a better whole

Who can leave the house in the morning
And have the faintest notion that this day
Before his tousled hair kisses his pillow goodnight
True love will knock upon his door and ask entrance

Though our heart beats behind our breastplate
Its ways are known only to itself
Its desires and yearnings painfully palpable
Yet its salvation hidden beyond our gaze

And our intellect refuses to stand idly by
Analyzing and dissecting at every opportunity
Too old. Too young. Too tall. Too short.
Too Talkative. Too quiet. And on and on.
Or perhaps worse yet deeming one worthy
Solely because of social status or wealth
And so we judge as if we know what we're about

Our emotions too make their play
How bewitching the laughing eyes
How beautiful her figure. How rugged his.
How gorgeous her face. How handsome his.
How powerful our soothsaying emotions
They can leave us swooning and panting for breath
And sadly many heed this sweet siren's song
Only to awaken too late and realize it but mirage
And the beauty that once seduced now reviles

But thru this churning ocean of chaos
Love can find its true course to the inner shores
Of two voyagers whose ships finally together port
Whether it be an unexpected rounding a bend
To be surprised by a breathtaking view
Or a gradual climb to the mountain's summit
And its anticipated panorama of beauty

There comes that special moment of the heart
Where all of life's nonessential trappings are peeled away
Where age, social stature, color, upbringing cease to exist
Where the clouded veil of accidental particulars is lifted
And the mind finally sees clearly what the heart has known

That moment when two hearts finally greet their owners
With happy news as intellects and passions rejoice
For now is passion fired purely
And intellect though it can explain it not
Knows truth when it is revealed

That moment when with their essences now fully exposed
Two souls greet each other bare and naked and pure
When heart and soul and passions in unison cry out
This is the one!

Aye! This *very* moment as I look into your eyes
And two souls unite

Thou art the flame

On the darkened canvas of night.
As the moon quietly sighs for the sun.
There flares a solitary flame.
Gently crackling, dancing in delight.

Thou art the flame

I dream of you all day.
All night I lay awake.
Calling for you in vain.
You must hear my cry!

Thou art the flame

To no avail. I try to eat. To sleep.
There is nothing of this world to inflame me.
Impassioned. There is nothing - only you.
I was meant to be thy fuel. Make me thine.

Thou art the flame

Let nothing of me remain. Nothing.
Nothing untouched by your flame.
Not a single thought. Not a strand of hair.
Not so much as a faded fingerprint.

Thou art the flame

I cast myself into your furnace -
Eager fuel to feed thy flames.
All I am. All I have. All I desire.
Consume me whole. Consume me.

Thou art the flame

Within your rapturous flames - no longer wood.
I am pulsing embers with ardor glowing.
Transformed. Permeated by; united with . . . you.
No longer me. Consumed by thee.

Thou art *my* flame

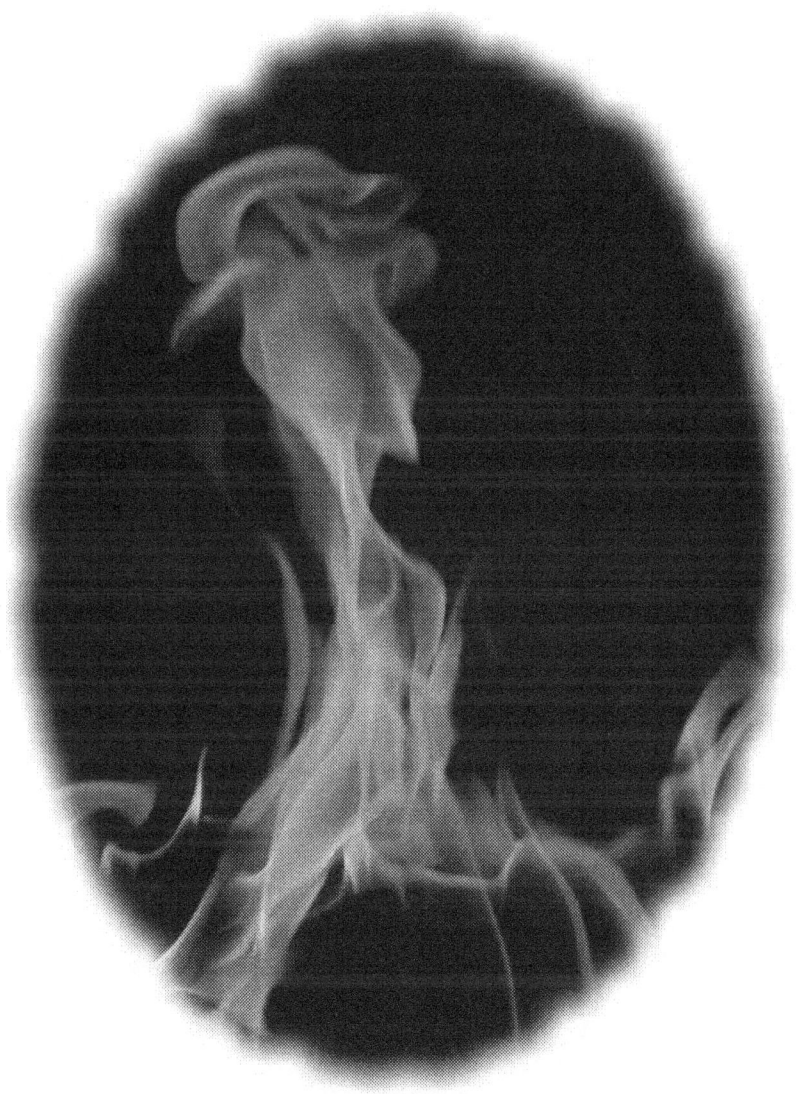

----- Appendix -----

Acrostic: a poetic form in which the first letters from every line combine to spell a word (or words). My example of an acrostic is *Captivated Maiden* on page 13.

Double Acrostic: a poetic form like the acrostic but in which the last letters of every line also combine to form an additional word (or words). Usually the letters at the beginning and end of the lines would be different and hence would spell different words. In my example, however, I added the twist of starting and ending each line with the same letter. So in my *Enchantress* on page 18, "Enchantress" is spelled twice.

Monchielle: a poetic form created by my friend, "Starhiker" from www.allpoetry.com. The first line repeats in each stanza. There are a total of four stanzas each consisting of five lines. Each line has six syllables. Line three and line five must rhyme. My example, *When I Awake* on page 42, is slightly different in that line four of each stanza also rhymes with lines three and five.

Shakespearean Sonnet: a 14 line poem with three verses of four lines each and a rhyming couplet at the end. It is written in iambic pentameter and has the rhyme scheme *abab cdcd efef gg*. *Silent Caresses,* a poem about love at first sight, on page 12 is my attempt at the noble Shakespeare's trademark form.

Greensleeves: *What Love Is This* on page 48 was written to the melody *Greensleeves* which is also the melody of one of my favorite Christmas carols, *What Child Is This*.